D0393897

Presented to:

_____

in honor of

your wedding day

From This Day Forward

A CELEBRATION OF MARRIAGE

ELLYN SANNA WITH RACHEL QUILLIN

A DAYMAKER GREETING BOOK

Hear the mellow wedding bells, —

Golden bells!

What a world of happiness their harmony foretells!

Through the balmy air of night

How they ring out their delight!

From the molten golden notes,

What a liquid ditty floats

To the turtle-dove that listens, while she gloats

On the moon!

Oh from out the sounding cells,

What a gush of euphony voluminously wells!

How it swells!

How it dwells

Oh the Future! How it tells

Of the rapture that impels

To the swinging and the ringing

Of the bells, bells, bells. . .

To the rhyming and the chiming of the bells!

EDGAR ALLAN POE, FROM "THE BELLS"

HOW DO I LOVE THEE?

LET ME COUNT THE WAYS. . . .

IF GOD CHOOSE,

I SHALL BUT LOVE THEE BETTER

AFTER DEATH.

ELIZABETH BARRETT BROWNING

THEREFORE SHALL A MAN LEAVE

HIS FATHER AND HIS MOTHER,

AND SHALL CLEAVE UNTO HIS WIFE:

AND THEY SHALL BE ONE FLESH.

GENESIS 2:24

I think you are good, gifted, lovely:
a fervent, a solemn passion
is conceived in my heart; it leans to you. . .
and, kindling in pure, powerful flame,
fuses you and me in one.

CHARLOTTE BRONTË

$\mathscr{I}$N LOVE,

THE PARADOX OCCURS

THAT TWO BEINGS BECOME ONE

AND YET REMAIN TWO.

ERICH FROMM

ACCEPT—

THE *S*ECRET

OF A GOOD

MARRIAGE

ATTRACTION

COMMUNICATION

COMMITMENT

ENJOYMENT

PURPOSE

TRUST

UNKNOWN

Marriage resembles a pair of shears,
so joined they cannot be separated;
often moving in opposite directions,
yet always punishing anyone who comes between them.

SYDNEY SMITH

Love is. . .born with the pleasure of looking at each other,

it is fed with the necessity of seeing each other,

it is concluded with the impossibility of separation!

JOSÈ MARTÌ Y PERÉZ

Come live with me, and be my love,
And we will some new pleasures prove
Of golden sands, and crystal brooks,
With silken lines, and silver hooks.

JOHN DONNE

To wed is to bring not only our worldly goods
but every potential capacity. . . .
In becoming one, these two create a new world
that had never existed before.

PAUL E. JOHNSON

Love gives us in a moment

what we can hardly attain

by effort after years of toil.

J. W. VON GOETHE

A successful marriage requires
falling in love many times,
always with the same person.

MIGNON MCLAUGHLIN

And now abideth faith, hope, charity, these three;

but the greatest of these is charity.

1 CORINTHIANS 13:13

"My well-beloved is mine and I am his."

Love was their banqueting-house,

love was their wine, love was their ensign. . .

love was his apples, love was her comforts;

love made him see her, love made her seek him;

love made him wed her,

love made her follow him; . . .

Love bred our fellowship,

let love continue it,

and love shall increase it until death dissolve it.

JOHN WINTHROP, TO HIS FIANCÉE

Love vanquishes time. To lovers,

a moment can be eternity,

eternity can be the tick of a clock.

MARY PARISH

Live joyfully with the wife whom thou lovest
all the days of the life.

ECCLESIASTES 9:9

Love makes those young whom age doth chill,

And whom he finds young, keeps young still.

PETER CARTRIGHT

And walk in love, as Christ also hath loved us,

and hath given himself for us an offering

and a sacrifice to God for a sweetsmelling savour.

EPHESIANS 5:2

Hope is like a harebell, trembling from its birth;
Love is like a rose, the joy of all the earth;
Faith is like a lily, lifted high and white;
Love is like a lovely rose, the world's delight.
Harebells and sweet lilies show a thornless growth,
But the rose with all its thorns excels them both.
CHRISTINA ROSSETTI

Behold, thou art fair, my love;
behold, thou art fair.
SONG OF SOLOMON 4:1

Love is the fairest bloom in God's garden.
UNKNOWN

Love is a symbol of eternity.

It wipes out all sense of time,

destroying all memory of a beginning

and all fear of an end.

ANNE-LOUISE-GERMAINE DE STAËL

O love, resistless in thy might,
thou triumphest even over gold!

SOPHOCLES

My life, my dear sweet life, my life-light, my all,

my goods and chattels, my castles, acres, lawns, and vineyards,

O sun of my life, sun, moon, and stars, heaven and earth,

> *my past*

and future, my bride, my girl, my dear friend. . .

> *my heart blood,*

my entrails, star of my eyes, O dearest, what shall I call you?

HEINRICH VON KLEIST

 LOVE YOU,

NOT BECAUSE YOU ARE PERFECT,

BUT BECAUSE YOU

ARE SO PERFECT FOR ME.

Unknown

I am my beloved's,
and my beloved is mine.

Song of Solomon 6:3

A wise lover values not so much the

gift of the lover

as the love of the giver.

Thomas À Kempis

Love comforteth
like sunshine after rain.

William Shakespeare

Beloved, let us love one another:

for love is of God; and every one that loveth

is born of God, and knoweth God.

1 John 4:7

Love does not consist in gazing at each other

but in looking together in the same direction.

ANTOINE DE SAINT-EXUPÉRY

Chains do not hold a marriage together.

It is threads, hundreds of tiny threads

that sew people together through the years.

SIMONE SIGNORET

No cord or cable can draw so forcibly,

or bind so fast,

as love can do with a single thread.

ROBERT BURTON

I WILL GREATLY REJOICE IN THE LORD,

MY SOUL SHALL BE JOYFUL IN MY GOD;

FOR HE HATH CLOTHED ME

WITH THE GARMENTS OF SALVATION,

HE HATH COVERED ME

WITH THE ROBE OF RIGHTEOUSNESS,

AS A BRIDEGROOM DECKETH HIMSELF

WITH ORNAMENTS, AND AS A BRIDE

ADORNETH HERSELF WITH HER JEWELS.

ISAIAH 61:10

For this cause shall a man leave his father and mother,

and shall be joined unto his wife, and they two shall be one flesh.

EPHESIANS 5:31

Marriage is not finding that person with whom you can live,

but finding that person with whom you cannot live without.

HOWARD HENDRICKS

Successful marriage is always a triangle:

a man, a woman, and God.

CECIL MYERS

Happy marriages begin when we marry the ones we love,

and they blossom when we love the ones we marry.

TOM MULLEN

*My heart
is ever at
your service.*

WILLIAM SHAKESPEARE

She is mine to have and to hold!

She has chosen

between love and gold!

All the joys life can give

Shall be hers, while I live,

For she's mine to have and to hold.

Will A. Heelan

Let the wife make her husband glad to come home,

and let him make her sorry to see him leave.

MARTIN LUTHER

Wherefore they are no more twain, but one flesh.
What therefore God hath joined together,
let not man put asunder.

MATTHEW 19:6

It is not your love that sustains the marriage,

but from now on, the marriage that sustains your love.

DIETRICH BONHOEFFER

Married life offers no panacea—
if it is going to reach its potential,
it will require an all-out investment
by both husband and wife.

JAMES C. DOBSON

Make us of one heart and mind,

Courteous, merciful, and kind;

Lowly, meek in thought and word,

Ne'er by fretful passion stirred.

Free from anger, free from pride,

Let us thus in God abide;

All the depth of love express,

All the height of holiness.

CHARLES WESLEY

Immature love says:

"I love you because I need you."

Mature love says:

"I need you because I love you."

ERICH FROMM

You learn to speak by speaking,
to study by studying, to run by running,
to work by working;
and just so you learn to love. . .by loving.
Begin as a mere apprentice,
and the very power of love will lead you
on to become a master of the art.

FRANCIS OF SALES

Love is not an affectionate feeling,

but a steady wish for the loved person's ultimate good

as far as it can be obtained.

C. S. LEWIS

❧ ———————————————————————————————— ❧

Love is like a friendship caught on fire.

In the beginning a flame, very pretty,

often hot and fierce but still only light and flickering.

As love grows older, our hearts mature,

and our love becomes as coals,

deep burning and unquenchable.

BRUCE LEE

Love is, above all, the gift of oneself.

JEAN ANOUILH

There is but one genuine love potion—
consideration.

MENANDER

Where love reigns the very joy of heaven itself is felt.

HANNAH HURNARD

Life is the flower of which love is the honey.

VICTOR HUGO

To love is. . .

what makes this world a garden.

ROBERT LOUIS STEVENSON

You ought to trust me for I do not love

and will never love any woman in the world but you,

and my chief desire is to link myself to you

week by week by bonds which shall ever

become more intimate and profound.

Beloved I kiss your memory—your sweetness

and beauty have cast a glory upon my life.

SIR WINSTON CHURCHILL,
TO HIS WIFE CLEMENTINE

Love is a mixture of honey and bitterness.

CISTERELLA

When you love someone,

all your saved-up wishes start coming out.

ELIZABETH BOWEN

The courage to share your feelings
is critical to sustaining a love relationship.

HAROLD H. BLOOMFIELD

Whoso loves believes the impossible.

ELIZABETH BARRETT BROWNING

The development
of a really good marriage
is not a natural process.
It is an achievement.

DAVID AND VERA MACE

Except the Lord build the house,

they labour in vain that build it.

PSALM 127:1

A happy marriage is the union
of two good forgivers.

ROBERT QUILLEN

THE SECRET

TO A LONG MARRIAGE

IS TO PUT A LITTLE

Romance

in every day.

UNKNOWN

Marriage is that relation
between man and woman
in which the independence is equal,
the dependence mutual,
and the obligation reciprocal.

LOUIS K. ANSPACHER

He's more myself than I am.

Whatever our souls are made of, his

and mine are the same. . . .

If all else perished and he remained,

I should still continue to be,

and if all else remained, and he were annihilated,

the universe would turn a mite stranger. . . .

He's always, always in my mind;

not as a pleasure to myself, but as my own being.

EMILY BRONTË, *WUTHERING HEIGHTS*

Intreat me not to leave thee,

or to return from following after thee:

for whither thou goest, I will go;

and where thou lodgest, I will lodge:

thy people shall be my people, and thy God my God:

Where thou diest, will I die, and there will I be buried:

the Lord do so to me, and more also,

if ought but death part thee and me.

RUTH 1:16–17

At home by the fire, whenever you look up, there I shall be—
and whenever I look up, there will be you.

THOMAS HARDY

The Christian is supposed to love his neighbor,

and since his wife is his nearest neighbor,

she should be his deepest love.

MARTIN LUTHER

Love is a great thing, a great and thorough good;
by itself it makes everything that is heavy light;
and it bears evenly all that is uneven.
It carries a burden which is no burden;
it will not be kept back by anything low and mean;
it desires to be free from all worldly affections,
and not to be entangled by any outward prosperity,
or by any adversity subdued.
Love feels no burden, thinks nothing of trouble,
attempts what is above its strength,
pleads no excuse of impossibility.
It is therefore able to undertake all things,
and it completes many things,
and warrants them to take effect,
where he who does not love would faint and lie down.
Though weary, it is not tired; though pressed,
it is not straitened; though alarmed,
it is not confounded; but as a living flame
it forces its way upward, and securely passes through all.
Love is active and sincere; courageous,
patient, faithful, and prudent.

THOMAS À KEMPIS

To believe in something not yet proved
and to underwrite it with our lives;
it is the only way we can leave the future open.

LILLIAN SMITH

Love gives itself; it is not bought.

HENRY WADSWORTH LONGFELLOW

It is a commitment of the will.
God wills to love us, come what may. . . .
To fall in love under God
is to share this quality with one's partner.

LIONEL A. WHISTON

Love alone is capable of uniting living beings

in such a way as to complete and fulfill them,

for it alone takes them and joins them

by what is deepest in themselves.

PIERRE TIELHARD DE CHARDIN

Marriage has in it less of beauty,

but more of safety, than the single life;

it has more care, but less danger;

it is more merry, and more sad;

it is fuller of sorrows, and fuller of joys;

it lies under more burdens,

but it is supported by

all the strengths of love, and charity,

and those burdens are delightful.

JEREMY TAYLOR

Love can be understood only "from the inside,"
as a language can be understood only by someone who speaks it,
as a world can be understood only by someone who lives in it.
ROBERT C. SOLOMON

Love is not like a reservoir.

You'll never drain it dry.

It's much more like a natural spring.

The longer and farther it flows,

the stronger and the deeper

and the clearer it becomes.

EDDIE CANTOR

When we reflect on the meaning of love,
we see that it is to the heart
what summer is to the farmer's year.
It brings to harvest
all the loveliest flowers of the soul.
BILLY GRAHAM

Now you will feel no rain

   for each of you will be shelter for the other;

Now you will feel no cold

   for each of you will be warmth for the other;

Now there is no more loneliness

   for each of you will be companion for the other;

Now you are two bodies

   but there is only one life before you;

Go now to your dwelling place

   to enter into the days of your togetherness,

And may your days be good and long upon the earth.

NATIVE AMERICAN BLESSING

He who loves something
mentions it very often.

ARABIAN PROVERB

EVER FORGET
THAT THE MOST
POWERFUL FORCE
ON EARTH IS LOVE.

Nelson Rockefeller

LOVE IS AN ACTION,

AN ACTIVITY.

IT IS NOT A FEELING.

M. SCOTT PECK

Put on therefore, as the elect of God, holy and beloved,

bowels of mercies, kindness, humbleness of mind, meekness, longsuffering;

Forbearing one another, and forgiving one another,

if any man have a quarrel against any:

even as Christ forgave you, so also do ye.

And above all these things put on charity, which is the bond of perfectness.

And whatsoever ye do in word or deed, do all in the name of the Lord Jesus,

giving thanks to God and the Father by him.

Wives, submit yourselves unto your own husbands, as it is fit in the Lord.

Husbands, love your wives, and be not bitter against them.

COLOSSIANS 3:12—14, 17—19

WHERE WE LOVE IS HOME,

HOME THAT OUR FEET MAY LEAVE,

BUT NOT OUR HEARTS.

WENDALL HOLMES

Love builds Bridges

WHERE THERE ARE NONE.

R.H. DELANEY

Intimacy. . .

the mystical bond of friendship,

commitment,

and understanding.

JAMES C. DOBSON

To love is to receive a glimpse of heaven.

KAREN SUNDE

My heart is like a singing bird. . .

Because the birthday of my life

Is come, my love is come to me.

Christina Rossetti

To have and to hold,

From this day forward

For better, for worse,

For richer, for poorer,

In sickness and in health,

To love and to cherish,

Till death us do part.

The Lord bless thee, and keep thee:

The Lord make his face shine upon thee,

and be gracious unto thee:

The Lord lift up his countenance upon thee,

and give thee peace.

Numbers 6:24–26

Congratulations!

on this exciting day of your life.

may god bless your marriage

in a very special way!

DayMaker
GREETING BOOKS

‹ 2003 by Barbour Publishing,
ISBN 1-58660-81

Cover Image ‹ Liz Banfield Workbookst
Book design by Kevin Keller | designconce

Unless otherwise noted, Scripture quotati
are taken from the King James Version of the Bi

Published by Barbour Publishing, I
P.O. Box 719, Uhrichsville, Ohio 44683. www.barbourbooks.c

Printed in Chi